T0012073

Bicycle Safety

VISTA®
HIGHER LEARNING

Boston, Massachusetts

SOCIAL STUDIES

Do you want to have fun on a bicycle?

It is time to ride your bike! *Bike* is another word for *bicycle*. You know how to ride a bike, but you need to know how to be safe on a bike, too.

Do you know how to be safe on a bike?

There are a few easy things you can do to stay safe on a bike. First, ask an adult to ride with you and help you stay safe. Then, you need to learn more about bike safety. What are some ways to be safe on a bike?

Do you have a safe bicycle?

Most bicycles today look like the safety bicycle from the 1880s. Both old and new bikes have two wheels that are the same size. They each have a **seat**, a **handlebar**, and a **brake**, too. The brake helps you stop the bicycle.

old safety bicycle

handlebar

seat

brake

new safety bicycle

Does your bike work?

Your bike needs to work well, so you need to check your bike before you ride. The wheels need to be on tight, the **tires** need to have air in them, and your brakes must work. Ask an adult to help you.

tires

Do you have a helmet?

A good **helmet** is important for bicycle safety because a helmet keeps your head safe. Find a good bike helmet, and make sure the helmet fits your head. Never ride a bike without a bike helmet.

helmet

Do you have bicycle lights and bright colors?

It is also important that other people can see you when you ride. So, use lights on your bike, and wear clothes with bright colors. Bike lights and bright colors help people in cars and on bikes to see you.

Do you have a bike bell?

You want other people to hear you, too. A bike bell helps people hear you when you are on your bike. When you ring the bell, it **warns** people you are riding near them.

ring

warns

Do you ride on a bike path?

Try to ride on a **bike path**. A bike path is a safe place for bikes because cars do not go on a bike path.

bike path

Do you see and hear cars and people?

You need to look and listen when you are on your bike. Your eyes and ears help to keep you safe. Look and listen for cars and people who are walking or riding on other bikes.

Do you know the weather?

Before you ride, know what kind of weather is coming. Try not to ride in rainy or stormy weather. It is hard to see cars in the rain, and it is hard for people in cars to see you in the rain.

Do you know the rules?

People in cars have to follow rules for driving. People on bikes need to follow rules, too. Look at signs on the street and signs on the bike path. Ask an adult to tell you the rules in your town or city.

Do you see the traffic light?

A traffic light is a **safety invention** that helps people in cars stay safe. It helps people walking and riding bikes, too. Stop when the light is red. Go when the light is green.

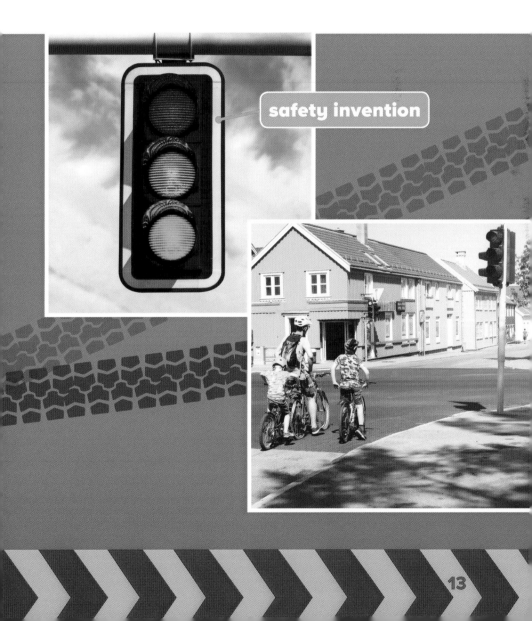

safety invention

Be safe!

Now you have read the answers to many questions about bicycle safety. You know how to be safe on a bike. You have a helmet, a bike bell, and bright clothes. You know the rules, and it's time to ride.

Have fun!

Get on your bike and follow the rules for bicycle safety. Stay on the bike path, listen and look for cars, and know what the weather is like. And there's one more rule. Have fun on your bike!

bike path

safety invention

brake

seat

handlebar

tires

helmet

warns